A Permeable Life
POEMS AND ESSAYS

By Carrie Newcomer

A Permeable Life

Copyright ©2013
Carrie Newcomer / Available Light Publishing
www.carrienewcomer.com

ISBN 978-0-615-90275-3

Book design by Hugh Syme

Photo by Jim Krause

Edited by Cate Whetzel

- CONTENTS -

- ESSAYS -

Preface

If you were to ask a collection of eleven songwriters how they write their songs, they will describe to you eleven different ways of going about it. Some songwriters start with the lyrics, some start with the music. Some songwriters write lyrics and music at the same time. But my process, more often than not, starts with an idea, a question, an experience. I write poetry and essays to find the shape and form of the thing, and from those writings my songs are born. This collection of poems and essays was written over the last several years. Most began as notes jotted down while walking in the woods, on long drives between here and there, in hotel rooms and on airplanes, in my own office, at diners, and backstage before shows. If you are familiar with my songwriting you may recognize themes or even a few lines that have shown up in my musical works. These poems and essays are about the natural world, the quality of light, and the invisible spirit that shines below the surface of all things. Some describe finding something sacred in what is absolutely ordinary. Some explore relationships and look at the world with a somewhat sideways sense of humor. Some are about my dogs.

I had a lot of fun putting together this collection, revisiting and remembering many of the places and experiences that became words, and then became music. I hope you enjoy this collection as well.

Carrie Newcomer

September 2013

Poetry

A Permeable Life

I want to leave enough room in my heart
For the unexpected,
For the mistake that becomes knowing,
For knowing that becomes wonder,
For wonder that makes everything porous,
Allowing in and out
All available light.

An impermeable life is full to the edges,
But only to the edges.
It is a limited thing.
Like the pause at the center of the breath,
Neither releasing or inviting,
With no hollow spaces
For longing and possibility,

I would rather live unlocked,
And more often than not astonished,
Which is possible
If I am willing to surrender
What I already think I know.
So I will stay open
And companionably friendly,
With all that presses out from the heart
And comes in at a slant
And shimmers just below
The surface of things.

In the Hayfield

Last evening,
As I drove into this small valley,
I saw a low-hanging cloud
Wandering through the trees.
It circled like a school of fish
Around the dun-colored hay bales.
Reaching out its foggy hands
To stroke the legs of a perfect doe
Quietly grazing in a neighbor's mule pasture.
I stopped the car
And stepping out into the blue twilight,
A wet mist brushed my face,
And then it was gone.
It was not unfriendly,
But it was not inclined to tell its secrets.

I am in love with the untamed things,
The cloud, the doe,
Water, air and light.
I am filled with such tenderness
For ordinary things:
The practical mule, the pasture,
A perfect spiral of gathered hay.
And although I should not be,
Consistent as it is,
I am always surprised
By the way my heart will open
So completely and unexpectedly,
With a rush and an ache,
Like a sip of cold water
On a tender tooth.

Three Gratitudes

This poem is related to the song "Thank You Good Night"

Every night before I go to sleep
I say out loud
Three things that I am grateful for,
All the significant, insignificant
Extraordinary, ordinary stuff of my life.
It's a small practice and humble,
And yet, I find I sleep better
Holding what lightens and softens my life
Ever so briefly at the end of the day.
Sunlight and blueberries,
Good dogs and wool socks,
A fine rain,
A good friend,
Fresh basil and wild phlox,
My father's good health,
My daughter's new job,
The song that always makes me cry,
Always at the same part,
No matter how many times I hear it.
Decent coffee at the airport,
And your quiet breathing,
The story she told me,
The frost patterns on the window,
English horns and banjos,
Wood Thrush and June bugs,
The smooth glassy calm of the morning pond,
An old coat,
A new poem,
My library card,
And that my car keeps running

Despite all the miles.

And after three things,
More often than not,
I get on a roll and just keep on going,
I keep naming and listing,

Until I lie grinning,
Blankets pulled up to my chin,
Awash with wonder
At the sweetness of it all.

A Heart of Light

You are unquenchable spirit,
A heart of Light
Called to make more
Than just an appearance.
Invited to show up
With your truest self,
Your deepest you,
Awake and uncovered,
Even with all the risk
Such intentional wholeness implies.

Why We Are Here

She stood looking out the doorway
Poised to step out into whatever comes next.
Although I knew that I could not go with her
I could keep her company while waiting,
Bear witness to the preparing,
And maybe rub her tired shoulders
Which I know is absolutely nothing
And absolutely everything,

Maybe that is why we are here:
To rub shoulders and play cards,
To be a place to launch,
And a place to land,
To murmur on the phone late at night,
And to say,
"This I love"
And
"This I saw."

The Blue Umbrella

Today I saw a woman
Fold up her blue umbrella
And step out into the rain.
She lifted her lovely face.
Soft,
So softly,
She closed her eyes and smiled.
Drops of water slipped down,
Running over and around
Her warm, grateful lids,
Sliding down her cheeks
Like unchecked tears.
After a moment or two
She walked on
(Without putting up her umbrella).
Leaving me beached and breathless,
Feeling as if I had just witnessed
Perhaps the finest prayer
Ever prayed.

Visitation

Sunlight, winter white,
Clean, clear, not a smudge of grey,
Nothing to dull it down or soften the blow,
So bold and audacious
That it quickens the breath
And startles the eye.

It is always the quality of light
That nearly flattens me with wonder.
Filling me up and spreading out like liquid,
Into the corners of my eyes,
All the way to the edges
Of my peripheral vision.

First we see from the center.
We notice what is obvious,
Although to grasp even that
May take some time.
But then, from there,
We begin to glimpse what lives at the margins,
Barely perceived,
Like a suggestion of color,
Or fine shade of meaning.

I love what I catch at the corners,
When I'm not looking at the thing directly,
Or even looking for it at all.
This is what delights me the most,
The pause, the moment
When there is a shift in the light,
A sudden blur of wings,
A movement in the snow,

And when I turn to see,
It is always gone,
Leaving me with only an intuition
Or impression
Of the briefest visitation.

Showing Up

You
Are holy
And sacred
And utterly unique.
There are gifts you were born to give.
Songs you were born to sing
Stories you were born to tell.
And if you do not give it,
The world will simply lose it.
It is yours alone to offer,
No one can give it for you.
And dearest,
Listen, because this is important,
This wounded world
Needs all the songs we can pull from the air,
Every story that helps us to remember.
It needs every single gift,
Large and small.
And yes,
Dearest,
This grateful world does rejoice
Every courageous time
We are true to ourselves and to our gifts.
And so it is,
Dear heart,
We embrace the song
And the story
And all our gifts
Because the world has such great need
And because the world exceedingly rejoices
And because there is no sadder thing
Than to leave this world

Having never really shown up.

Remembering

I am remembering
My unbroken self,
Which understands that silence
Can be considered an absence of sound,
Or experienced as a fullness of spirit.

I am remembering
That all is vanity in the end,
Except for the love that tumbles out of us,
Or shines down upon us,
In fleeting, glowing moments.
I am remembering
My own wholeness,
The perfect soul I was born with,
Assessing my long endeavors to name the unnamable,
And describe what I know only from the corner of my eye.

I am remembering a lifetime of trying to map
The shape of shadow and light,
To draw the clean edges of change.
And what has made me an oddity
Asked me to live far more closely
To the center of all that awe and ache.

I am remembering my promise,
My willing decision to stand
In a shaft of January light,
Fascinated by the shimmer of the dust,
Suspended in a quiet room,
And how the light travels across the floor,

As a short day lengthens,
Reaching out like hands,
Covering the wood planks like spilled water.

Becoming

Water becomes rain,
And then becomes stream,
Which then becomes river,
Becomes ocean,
Becomes mist,
Becomes fog,
Becomes rain,
Which slides down the rocks,
And is taken into the ground,
And then taken up by the plants,
Animals and birds and people.
It becomes the sweat of the brow,
And the tears slipping down,
Upon a shirt that has been slept in.
Evaporating into air,
It remains invisible for a while. Then,
After a time,
It becomes dew which burns off
As the liquid sun rises,
Becoming mist,
Becoming cloud,
Becoming rain.
Nothing is ever really gone,
It only transforms.

The Fox and the Dog

In the gloaming,
In the blue hour,
As the last moments of light
Slipped below the ridge top,
And beyond the knowable horizon,
I sat on the porch steps,
Barn jacket and boots,
With my old dog leaning
For solace and balance
Into my shoulder.
She laid her grey head
At the vulnerable hollow
At the base of my throat,
And heaved a great sigh,
For even dogs are affected
By this kind of beauty,
Which continually presents itself
Whether we are paying attention or not.

Just then,
In that long exhale of the day,
A fox, still clothed in thick winter fur,
Emerged from between the trees
At the wood line just above the garden.
It sat down on the new grass and old leaves
And silently gazed at the pair of us there.
This is a rare thing to see a fox just so,
For these creatures are private and wild
And most often seen (if seen at all)
As a proud flash of red or vanishing flanks.

The fox and the dog considered one another
Without longing or regret,
The wild and the loyal,
Content in their choices to be utterly
And completely true.
"I am fox, and I could not have been more fox than I am."
"I am dog, and I could not have been more faithfully dog."
And with a nod of tribute
And the rolling of red ears,
And lowering of white lashes,
In the very last flash of the setting sun,
The fox walked away.
He did not look back
Leaving an open space
Shaped like a question mark.

To the Ridge Top

She doesn't see so well
And her hearing is not good.
Her back legs are tired,
Curved by an advancing arthritis.
A trip to the mailbox and back
Has become too much.
But tonight,
On this spring evening,
She caught a scent on the air
And her soft old ears lifted
And she leaned out into something
She could not see or hear,
But sensed with a powerful calling.

She roused her achy old bones
And headed out with a purpose,
With doglike determination,
Walking stiffly but quickly
Up the long winding path
Which starts at the backdoor
And leads to the ridge top.
Where you can see the dappled sun set.

The hill is covered with muddy growing things
And barely clothed maples, beeches and ash.
It's a steep path and a hard one,
Even if you are used
To walking the hills of southern Indiana
And even more so for a crippled old dog.
I called her,

A bit worried,
Remembering her last walkabout
At 2:00 am in the February snow.
Following her down to the barn
And carrying her home
When her weary legs simply gave out.

But tonight
She has a mission,
She is inspired by the energy of spring
Buoyed up by a newness
That is filling the world.
A horned owl beckoned
From across the hollow,
The pond peepers cheered her on,
And I followed behind in my boots and pajamas,
Catching her purpose, sharing her excitement.
And as she walked out onto the ridge
There in the last light,
She lifted her elegant white nose
And faced quietly
Into that rose and blue glow,
So satisfied,
So beautiful,
So completely alive.

It is not always easy getting old,
And yet there are moments
Of great energy,
Wonder,
And considerable magic,
When we release all that was
And embrace all that is.

That is when we catch a hint
Of something fine on the air
Something you might have missed
In the perpetual motion of youth.
But now you can sense it
With power and presence,
And you'll climb with a passion
To the top of a ridge
Just to catch the scent of it
Out there on the horizon.
Eventually we walked
Albeit more slowly
Back down the path and sat on the porch,
Where I smoothed her soft face
And rubbed her tired legs,
And we were happy,
So happy
In the twinkling dark.

Dharamsala

This poem was the starting point for the song "Writing You a Letter"

India, 2010

There were prayer wheels
Lining the monastery path.
I followed a friend,
Who was following an elderly man,
Who was following a young woman.
All of us touching and turning
Wooden pegs as soft as new skin,
As smooth as old stones.
Each turn was a prayer,
For all that we love,
For all that we've lost,
Calling in a kinder world,
Because kindness is yet a possibility.
On the far side of the monastery
The air was filled with the sound of moving fabric,
Countless prayer flags lifted in the mist.
It was like music,
Light and fleeting,
Lingering in the quiet,
Filling the world with longing
And our own good intentions.

At the final bend, an elderly nun
Showed me the correct way to bow three times,
Turn to the right, and receive a blessing.
"Don't worry that you are not Buddhist,
We don't care,
We bless everyone,"

She said, and stooped to bless a green lizard,
Gently encouraging him off the path.

Later, sitting in a sidewalk cafe,
I had a Pepsi,
Drank it out of a glass bottle with a straw.
Monks from the monastery
Moved through the streets
In maroon and yellow robes.
They were talking on cell phones
And wearing Crocs,
Apparently the spiritual footwear of choice.

Then the street started filling
With murmurs and expectation.
I was told the Dalai Lama
Would soon pass this way.
And by the side of the road
The old men counted prayer beads,
The young women lit incense,
Bouncing babies on their hips.
And when his car finally appeared
(An unadorned Honda)
As he slowly rolled by,
Every one of us bowed.
Every one of us leaned forward.
Hippie girls wearing dreadlocks,
Hindu women in saris,
A Sikh man in a turban,
A guy in a Gap T-shirt.
A middle aged couple in good hiking boots.
We were whispering in Tibetan,
German and English,

Thinking in Spanish, Russian and French.
The devoted, the blessed,
The lost and confused,
We were all leaning forward
Leaning out into hope,
Leaning out with a longing
To touch something better,
To touch something kinder
That might hold together;
Leaning forward
Into something
We could not even name.

Beneath the Flame Tree

Bits of this poem show up in the song "Everybody's Got Something"

Africa, June 2012

A tall elegant man
Stands beneath the flame tree
Out behind a small school
Speaking first in the mother tongue,
Then in Swahili,
Then in English.
He says, "Beloved, we are blessed."
Yes, here in this brutally beautiful place
Where a generation has been eaten
By a carnivorous virus
He says, "We are blessed."
To the frail grandmother who has taken in
Six neighborhood children,
And to the woman who has lost her husband
And who is now raising her sister's four children
With four of her own.
He says this to the great grandmama
With wrists as thin as papyrus reed,
He says this to a proud, thin tall man with milky eyes,
And to the woman who sells chapati in the village.
He says, "We are blessed"
To the man who breaks his back
Breaking the hard earth
With a hand shovel and sharpened hoe.
"We are blessed,
Because we today come together
And today the children eat,
And today the children are in school

And today the children are learning
And Beloved, this is hope."

Then
He explains to each one of us,
(And this is important)
That they ask all the children
Saved, truly saved,
By a simple school lunch program
To turn around and to give a little bit
From their little bit.
They tell them to give to the hollow-eyed children
Standing beyond the schoolyard,
The children even further outside than themselves.
Then he nods his head
And says, "Beloved, we are proud of our children,
Because each and every one,
Each and every one
Did this thing,
Not holding back
Even a little,
For this is the true nature of hope,
To do what you can do,
When it must be done."
At the sound of the music
The children came running
Across the soccer field,
An ocean wave of small feet and small shoes,
Some with holes in their sweaters
And green uniforms.
Arriving breathless and smiling,
To sit and sing with the elders
Beneath a flaming tree.

Luminous Things

or Where Does a Good Idea Go?
Middle East, 2013

I nudge a rock with my shoe as a battered
Toyota billows by.
Clouds of dust hang like a shroud,
Like a floating desert in the dry heat.
This is the place where the world leans in
To catch a glimpse,
To snatch a look,
Like hungry paparazzi,
Waiting for that money moment,
When something salaciously holy happens.

This is where every wall wavers in the unyielding sun,
Shimmering like a mirage of meaning,
Holding jealously the last shreds of visions,
And stranded remnants of wisdom,
Spoken by soft-voiced revolutionaries,
And hard-eyed prophets,
Who had nothing and everything to lose,
Who came riding in (willingly and unwillingly)
Consistent and spot on,
In their assessment of our tendency
And supremely human ability,
To steadfastly
And faithfully
Totally miss the point.
As the dust settles around me,
I breathe in the cold ash of a fire long gone
Which no amount of stirring manages to kindle

Into a new source of light or warmth,
And I cannot help but wonder,
What became of all those dreams that the old men dreamed,
And where did the visions of all those young girls go?
But yet,
But still,
I can imagine (unlikely as it might be)
That beautiful and luminous things
Do last beyond any one singular horizon.
And that is when in my heart's eye,
Which sees only from the edges,
I catch the flash and flight of a lovely idea
As it rises into the air and scatters across the sky.
It is as light and strong as a beating wing
Traveling over so many miles and for so many years
Landing and looking
Like doves to some and pigeons to others,
On telephone wires and window ledges,
Low branches and fresh-turned fields,
Cafes and carports,
Calling,
And calling,
And calling again,
In those strange
And comforting tones.

Singing in the Kitchen

My mother sang with full abandon
With the kitchen radio
When she was washing dishes.
She liked the old songs,
And she'd swing her hips,
Sashaying as much as a woman can
When elbow-deep in soapy water.
I would sit on the hardwood steps
Filled with pride and wonderment,
Whispering into my dog's ear,
With sage five year-old assurance,
"My mother has the voice of an angel."
As I recall, my dog agreed.

Years later,
Standing side by side on Sunday morning,
I was horrified,
In the way only a teenager can be horrified
When her mother is singing
Loudly and confidently,
Completely and consistently
Off key,
In church,
In public,
In front of her friends.

But now I understand
That my mother was a cautious soul,
Private and intentional,
And so I am grateful

That she taught me how to hold my little sister's hand
And look both ways before I crossed the street.
But I am also thankful
That either she did not know,
Or she did not care,
That her voice was not smooth or perfectly pitched.
She sang anyway,
Because some things just have to be
Exactly what they are,
And a song must be sung
One way or another.

Addition

My father taught me about numbers,
How to carry forward
What had grown too large for its column
Add the 5 to the 7
Carry forward the 10
Leaving only a 2.
It is like that,
Taking all you've come through,
Combining everything gathered and lost,
Add to the sum a little kindness
For doing the best you could
With what you knew at the time.
Tally up all the fives and sevens,
All the sixes and fours,
All that came up odd or even,
Then carry forward
Your expanded self
Which has grown beyond the limits
Of the first container.
Nothing is ever truly gone;
It only changes places.

The Stories We Tell

She said, "Did that really happen?"
And I answered,
"Of course it did.
Or at least almost.
This is the way it should have or might have
Or needed to have happened.
And to the best of my knowledge,
And by my most reliable memories,
This is how I understand it
To have been
And was
And still is."

She looked at me askance,
Not sure whether to follow the question,
Further down an obvious rabbit hole,
Or to simply believe me,
And leave it at that,
Not pressing to know
If the story was real
Or merely true.

Knowing

There are some questions,
There are some answers,
The simple ones,
The most important ones,
That cannot be approached
Or even seen,
Until we go out looking,
For something else entirely.

There is a note to ourselves,
That will not be found
Until we have searched
For everything new under the sun,
Until we have followed a hunch,
And braved enough hope,
Traced many necessary
And unnecessary
Public and private passages
Out to their natural ends.

Only when we return
To where we began,
Bringing home
All that the world has poured in,
And all we have poured out,
Can we lift the lid
Of the box on the mantel
Still there, where we left it,
At the start of it all.
And then
We can read

The unadorned writing
Traced on rough paper,
As holy as parchment,
And then
Only then
Can we carefully fold it
Place the words in our pocket
Right there
Over our heart.

A Box Turtle Lays Her Eggs

In my garden,
A box turtle the size of my open hand
Leaned into her digging,
First the back right leg,
And then the back left leg,
Reaching gracefully with her long curved toes,
Tenderly hollowing a safe place
To lay her four perfectly white,
Beautifully elongated
Rubbery eggs.
She would not be distracted
Or altered from her mission.
Now was the time to give her young
All she would ever give them.
Here was the place,
Between the calla lilies and the tuberoses
To bury her finest work.
She refilled the hollow with gentle dirt,
Carefully arranged the mulch
So that no person or raccoon or any un-turtle thing
Would perceive the ground
Had ever been disturbed.
She finished with as much of a sigh
As a box turtle can muster
And lumbered off into the tall grass
Never to return to what she so carefully placed.
In three months
Four turtles,
Each the size of a quarter,
Will dig their way to the surface,

And make a dash for the woods.
Unless the ground is too cold
Or the conditions not correct,
And then they will winter over,
Emerging in the spring.
Such sound judgment for creatures
Yet unborn
To sense it is infinitely wiser
To wait patiently under the snow
Until the time is right.
I get impatient,
I want to do something,
I want to fix the problem,
But I am inspired by the
Practicality and discretion
Of these honorable creatures.
I'm encouraged by the sagacious turtle
To be more determined,
To be righteous in my goals
And heave a big sigh after a job well done.
But then to have the good sense to know
When it's time to dig in,
Time to create,
Time to walk away,
Time to winter over,
Time to burst into the world,
Time to run for the woods,
Time to be no more or less
Than exactly what I am.

Holiday Checkout Line

She had pushed the same items across the scanner all day.
Cans of cranberry jelly,
Celery, bread crumbs and green beans,
Turkey and sweet potatoes,
Pumpkin pie mix and condensed milk.
An endless line of holiday shoppers waiting,
Shuffling from one foot to the other.
She looked weary, bone tired
But still, her sure hands moved
Quickly and efficiently over the scanner.
Beep, beep, beep.
"It's really amazing to think about," I said,
Beep, beep.
"How many Thanksgiving dinners
Have passed through your hands."
Beep, beep, beep.
"You've touched them all."
Beep, beep.
She looked up and with a little smile said,
"You know, I suppose you're right."
"That's a lot of love to send on its way," I said.
"Yes, it kinda is."
Then she tucked a stray hair behind her ear,
Straightened her shoulders and back.
And for a long lovely second,
It was like a veil had pulled away,
And we could see something
That was beautiful
And fine.

New Math

My father taught me
How to add and subtract fractions.
I had been sitting at the kitchen table
Discouraged and defeated.
"New Math" was destined
To be eventually labeled
An educational fad gone wrong,
Leaving an entire generation
Unable to do basic math functions
Without feeling vaguely
Apprehensive and distrustful.
My father's way worked better,
A fine bit of magic
Learned when he was only a boy
Before New Math.
He showed me how to see the patterns
And how find a common denominator,
Which are valuable skills,
Elegant and ecumenical.
I failed that particular homework assignment
Because I did not show my work
In the correct New Math symbols,
And this is how I learned
What the world really wants
Is not elegance or questions,
But a container to show
Your uniform answers.

Later,
At a university known

For producing fine engineers,
I took a seminar entitled "Math for Art Majors."
Curriculum experts believed it was important
For those of us who had failed New Math
To become reacquainted with the things
That we feared most.
I brought drawing pencils to class.
I sketched our TA's pale face,
His high forehead and longish side parted hair,
Early male pattern baldness
Of more far reaching interest
Than the factors and formulas
On the overhead projector.
To be honest I did enjoy the prime numbers.
I sensed family and kinship
With those quirky black sheep integers,
Numbers that do not fold nicely or evenly
Into anything other than themselves.
For hadn't I often eaten alone in cafeteria?
Hadn't I been laughed at
For reading the encyclopedia?
Hadn't I been told by a biology teacher
That the great biblical flood had been scientifically proved,
And that dinosaurs bones were part
Of a vast government plot?
Hadn't I been reprimanded
For my teary distress
At the thought of a God
Who would allow all those small birds
To fly and fly with no place to land,
Imagining how the poor things
Must have finally

Laid themselves down upon the dark water
To be swallowed by that newly made ocean.

At the same university
I took a class called "The Physics of Music"
(Which was not about music at all),
But instead about how sound
Moves through invisible air,
And methods of charting
Those unseen waveforms.
I asked my flushed professor
If anyone had ever tried to measure
The difference in coloration
Between bright sounds and shadows?
Had anyone documented the actual volume
Of the mysterious spirit
Contained in a haunting melody?
Has anyone ever tried to measure the weight
Of that which is wordless
In the words of a really fine song?
He didn't answer.
There was no common denominator.
I was obviously a prime number.
New Math written
All over my face.

Whaddayahavehon

This is the original poem from "Betty's Diner"

She dabs a pencil
on her tongue
"Whaddayahavehon?"
I'll have
a red plastic covered menu,
coffee and a piece of pie,
a radio humming
back in the kitchen
something about love
and loss,
a chalkboard announcing
fried chicken
with three vegetable sides:
green beans,
corn,
and applesauce.
I'll have
a long clean counter,
the click and clatter of silverware,
with the shush and slide of plates,
accompanied by the reliable hiss
of water running in and through
an ancient but faithful coffee machine.
I'll have
an endless sibilant assortment
of casual confidences
and daily specials,
a lone street lamp
outside a wide steamy window,
light falling like forgiveness

from unexpected sources,
a beacon
for all and any
regulars and refugees.

The Dare

or What Pushes Back

There is a voice
The one that speaks
With warm breath,
Close to our ear.
A voice that whispers in our most vulnerable moments
"You have simply not measured up."
"You could or should have gone further,
Burned brighter,
Been a whole lot less flawed."
This voice does not take into account
The strength of your love
Or depth of your longing.
It does not acknowledge
That you have braved so much
All the large and small
Public and private
Intentional acts of love.
It does not give you credit
For following your heart
When it would have been so much easier
To have followed the safe or inconspicuous.
This voice comes in the dark times
It pushes back at the very moment
You are trying hardest to move forward.
And when that voice is at its most desperate
It will simply say, "How dare you?"
"How dare you,
So human,
So flawed,
Who has made so many mistakes,

Claim the goodness of your heart,
Rest in the assurance of your best intentions?
How dare you try
Or claim,
Or ever rest?"
But we brave this voice,
This voice so like a buffeting wind,
A battering of words that we saw coming
Like the shadow of a storm across a wide field.
We pass through the center of the whirlwind,
Rake our fingers through our hair,
And raise up our heads
Saying with appreciation
And more than a little wonder,
"Yes, I have dared with
Courageous shaky knees."
"Yes, I have hoped and tried and failed
And hoped and tried again."
"Yes, I have risked everything,
Opened and poured my heart
Into the unsure container of the world."
"Yes, how I have dared,
Yes, how I have loved."
 Square back our shoulders
And dare again.

Because There Is Not Enough Time

I used to think
That because life is short
I should do more
Be more
Squeeze more
Into each and every day.
I'd walk around with a stick ruler
With increasing numbers
As the measure of fullness.

But lately
I've sensed
A different response
To a lack of time.
Felt in my bones
The singular worth
Of each passing moment.
Perhaps the goal
Is not to spend this day
Power skiing atop an ocean of multitasking.
Maybe the idea is to swim slower
Surer
Dive deeper
And really look around.
There is a difference between
A life of width
And a life of depth.

The Titmouse

On the bitter winter ground
I found a small grey titmouse
With a broken wing.
As I stopped to consider
How I might help her,
It became apparent
That something else
Was also broken inside her,
And that she was dying.

It is the way of the world,
One animal will eat another animal,
And all animals,
(Including the human kind),
Eventually go back into the earth.
And yet
I could not leave her there,
To die alone in the snow.

I cradled her in my mittened hands
And warmed her with my breath,
Trying to make her
As comfortable as possible.
I hummed to her
And breathed a silent prayer
To the god of snow and spring
and small birds.

After a while, her eyes drifted closed.
She did not struggle or appear afraid.

She was beyond that now,
She was just infinitely tired
And wise,
In the way that things
Approaching a great mystery
Are often wise.

Essays

Three Times

Bits of this essay show up in a song called "Abide"

Three times this winter I walked my old dog, Sophie, to the veil between this world and the next. But each time we stood at the threshold, she lifted her greying head, looked at the thing, and thought better of it. She peered into the mystery and decided to walk back to her memory foam bed, and her daily walks to the creek and meadow just beyond the barn. It has been a hard winter for an old dog, the cold and ache of the season settling into her tired bones. For sixteen years (Sophie is nearly 592 in dog years), she has placed her forehead against my chest, pressing it to the warmth and sturdiness of my sternum in quiet communion. With each near death excursion my heart has felt the wailings of loss. Each time I said goodbye and told her it was all right to let go. Each time I have assured her that she'd done everything a good dog could possibly do in one life. But each time she has said, "Oh God of meadows and woods and good dogs, grant me one more walk in the green, one more good sniffing of the meadow, one more pressing of my forehead in wordless love." And each time the God of meadows and woods and good dogs has heard and answered with a kindly, "Yes, this time."

I've learned a lot from this old friend, who without embarrassment or shame has asked me three times to walk with her to the edge of eternity, and then walk back. She takes help and does not feel she is unworthy or ashamed of receiving what is given in love. She has no ledger sheet of give and take. How hard it is for me to ask for help, even when I sorely need it. I worry about imposing. I wonder if I'm putting too much on that side of the accounts. In my darkest days, I have even feared I did not deserve such generosities. She lets me help. She allows me to feel useful and present with her, which enlarges my life and enlarges my spirit. This is a reminder to me that giving and receiving are not two sides of a coin, but rather interlocking pieces of a complete and whole heart.

She is grateful, and when her ability to run and swim left her, she was happy to walk, and then to walk slower. She does not grieve what she does not have. She loves what is directly in front of her. She does not miss the show worrying whether or not she has the best seat. How many times did I hold tight long beyond the time to let go? How many times have I mistakenly equated what I have with who I am? The life of a dog is now. A dog is grateful for what is, which I am finding to be the soundest kind of wisdom and very good theology.

In the taking of these three journeys, I have observed in myself an increasing inner calm and quietness of spirit. Our first trip to the doorway was filled with the buzzing white noise of grief. The second trip was very much the same. On the third trip I started to hear something beyond the buzzing, a clear space, as quiet and smooth as still water. At first I thought I might be becoming numb. How much white noise can a person sustain until the ears must be covered? But this calm is not about me closing down, but rather, opening up to her last gift to me. I have passed through the white noise of loss and the human desire to grasp and hold on to her. I have watched her go to the river, dip in a toe and walk back – but not because she was afraid of what was to come, or felt entitled to more. She walked back simply because it was not yet time. In the fullness of time we will all cross the river, and life gives us no guarantees to when or how this will happen. But this old friend has shown me how to sit in the sun, how to take one more walk in the green, enjoy one more good sniffing of the meadow. She has shown me how to love the now and be grateful for what is, and catch a glimpse of the shining brightness of daily things, which can only be seen in the awareness of limited time.

She has shown me a calm and quiet place where I can press my own weary head into the welcoming sternum of something made wholly of Light.

Time Is Kinder to Poets than Rockers

This essay was the starting point for a song called "Every Little Bit of It"

Los Angeles, 2013

Recently I had the opportunity to attend the largest music gear and instrument trade show in the country. I had been invited to attend this conference by a couple of old friends who happen to be two of the more renowned experts in early human history and stone age tools, and who also happen to love rock and roll, guitars and gear. When you think about it, it does make sense that these two Stone Age scientists would be fascinated with music gear and instruments, for these things are essentially the offspring and modern outcome of what was started so long ago in the form of stone axes, arrowheads, clay vessels and log drums. Their first motivation is about the love of music, of course, but it's joined by a love for the tools and items we human beings continue to make with our hands. We still turn metal, wood, plastic, string, and the modern synthetic equivalent of goatskin drum heads into tools humans used to create that communal, primal energy called rock and roll. I happen to love tools myself. I can get lost in a hardware store for hours thinking about what kind of sculpture I could build with this unusual metal fob, interesting bolt, or elegant bend of plumbing pipe. What treasure could I create with that hammer, a collection of strong mason tools or a penknife and key grinder. An art supply store can claim my attention indefinitely, with its shelves of neatly laid out brushes, pencils, paper and paint, rendering me nearly helpless with potential. I can also get lost for long periods of time in a good cooking store, with their walls of tools for very specific and sometimes esoteric food preparations. And, being a musician, I have a deep love and appreciation for a finely built instrument. Admittedly I'm not so fascinated by music gear. But the tool thing I totally get. So at the invitation of these true believers of the evolutionary place and significance of modern musical tools and their makers, I went to the Los Angeles NAMM convention.

Upon arrival a person is first stopped still by the sheer size of the show, covering what would amount to four floors, each the size of a couple of football fields, filled absolutely to bursting with booths and displays. Each booth, large or small, has been set up by individuals and companies trying to sell their music-related products to store owners, gear dealers, wholesale instrument distributors, school music programs, sundry rock bands and individual artists. These booths display a wide variety of all the physical stuff that surrounds the creation and presentation of music in all genres and forms (albeit in the L.A. location there is an obvious focus on the rock and heavy metal genre). There are booths displaying fine hand-built instruments, beautifully tooled Humbucker pickups, a whole floor of cheap knockoffs from China, acres of guitar amplifiers, computerized recording equipment, cellos, violins, banjos, ocarinas, whole show rooms of Bösendorfer pianos, concert sound systems complete with grinding Flying V guitars and Marshall stacks, Pro Tools mixing boards, computerized light shows and a high school auditorium-sized stage set up for showing off concert sound gear systems by a company called Peavey, which had hired greeters (kind of like Walmart senior greeters) but in this case at the door a cloud of smiling, nubile young women dressed in tiny leather skirts and halter-tops, thigh high fishnet stocking, black and red stilettos, draped in silver chains and crowned with the requisite long straight glossy back or platinum hair, handed out brochures to the crowd.

There were established owners and makers of revered brands present, who shook hands and met their appreciative public. There were the new makers and owners, who hoped their new tools would be the next preferred brand of the upwardly crankin' rock elite. There was

---

sales staff dressed appropriately for the wares on display, and working musicians in every other booth, hired to come in and play the impressive instruments. I have to tip my hat to those musicians. It was a tough gig for sure, playing covers of Journey and Styx tunes on the deafening showroom floor, rocking their hearts out while people wandered by. DJs were scratching away, and celebrity gods of heavy metal endorsed products, signing drumheads and glossy photos of themselves posed with instruments, effect pedals, and hot women. I even saw a man at a Goth rock gear booth dressed in a costume that looked half-Transformer, half-anime robot wizard, complete with platform vinyl boots, scary stegosaurus spines capping his shoulders, a *Silence of the Lambs* mask, and topped off by what appeared to be silver underpants, doing photo ops with passersby in front of a row of guitar cases shaped like coffins. There was a cacophony of sound, light and studded jackets at this show totally dedicated to buying, selling and celebrating the gear that promises to make you famous, help you play faster, better and harder. There were sales people working the shows, Japanese electronics guys in suits, journalists with cameras and interviewers camped out in media booths. There were former roadies selling heavy-duty wheeled road cases, and there were the bewildered and slightly overwhelmed observers like myself. I found myself most fascinated by the musicians not working the show but attending the whole glorious carnival, two hundred thousand rockers on parade. Eventually I just sat down on the ground, back to the wall, to take in this wild procession of humanity that almost defies description. This is when I was glad I am an aging folk singer and poet and not an aging rock and roller. It's hard enough getting older in an entertainment/music genre that still thinks learning a song from an old guy with no teeth in the hills of Appalachia is a badge of coolness. It's hard enough trying to remain relevant in your art, when you know that everything has been said before and probably with the same chord progression. Hard enough to continue to make songs, to keep at it because this is the work of your heart and soul, and because you believe that the most important things can be said more than once, and from different perspectives. It's hard enough to know that even though the old guy with no teeth in Appalachia is cool, that as a woman in entertainment you still need to stay thin enough to be taken for younger at a distance.

But rock and roll is all about youth, beauty, excess and pleasure. Rock and roll is about sex, and those engaged in rolling and rockin' are young and smooth and restless, they are tough and daring, they don't have double chins or kids at home. They hook up with groupies and other rockers; they don't hook up the DVD or Apple TV units to the cable box. In a crowd of unnumbered rockers, there were many musicians who fit all above-mentioned necessary criteria, but there were also what seemed to be about an 80% ratio older rockers to younger rockers. I saw women dressed in Cher-singing-on-the-Navy-transport gelled ringlets. There were women whose muffin tops had grown to fully baked family-sized loaves of white bread, women who had figured out their sexiest feature (or what 15 years ago had been their sexiest feature) and were exploiting it with an air of wild abandon. There were insanely huge breasts pushed up and falling out of leather corsets, long slender legs striding out from skirts that barely covered falling derrières. There were young rocker men who were sultry and trying to look bored (and failing) in their impossibly skinny black jeans and hipster glasses, Hispanic guys in low slung pants, baseball caps and tattoos that reached from shoulder to wrist, southern rockers in skull and crossbones wife-beater T-shirts and camouflage pants. But again, walking down the hallways with their rocker girlfriends rambled the 80% older rocker dudes. These were men who were still wearing long, fling-able White Snake hair and Dr. Martens. Some were wearing 80's Mötley Crüe eyeliner. Some were going bald, and had opted for the shaved head with the long goatish beard look. They ambled, decked out in black and black and more black, but instead of displaying the bare-chested sweaty allure of their twenties, they had taken on the tough sinewy look of too many drugs, or the comfortable and friendly spread of too many years of too much beer. I was a bit overwhelmed with the whole parade of many hopeful musicians, long past their rock-n-roll prime, trying to fit into the tight pants and bustiers of their glory days. It was like watching thousands of grown adults doing the middle age morning mirror gaze, the sideways glance, best angle, I-don't-really-have-a-chicken-neck-yet, appraisal. The only difference is that most of us do our sidelong glances in the privacy of our own blue-tiled bathrooms.

The next morning, waiting for my flight at LAX, I pulled out my paperback of Mary Oliver's poetry. Mary Oliver, who is now in her 80's, seems only to get more vibrant as she ages. Her poetry is filled with images from the natural world, reflections of life and grief, unnamable mystery, and the curious process of aging. She asks all the right questions, and doesn't tend to give any specific answers. I underlined several verses, and dog-eared three pages: "Hallelujah, I'm not where I started"; "I believe in kindness, also in mischief. Also in singing, especially when it is not necessarily prescribed"; and, "What we love, shapely and pure, is not to be held, but to be believed in, and then they vanish into the unreachable distance." I read these words of poetry about the musings of a life lived with more attention to depth and breadth rather than height. I thought about how I'd watched that parade of aging rockers with a little uncomfortable embarrassment, but glad the experience had been without sadness, for a life lived for a passion and art is never a sad thing, just sometimes a glorious and difficult thing (especially in tight leather pants). There was a good-sized part of me thinking, "You go, girl! Rock it and flaunt it like only a woman who has done some living can." And no, that little bit of embarrassment never went so far as pity, since pity would mean I was personally above such follies and miscalculations, which I am not, which I say smiling, which deepens my mouth lines. For one thing, I've found that after careful years of publicity photo sessions and

Photoshop we have now entered an era when every person you meet has a camera phone that can take uncorrected photos of you, and could Instagram, Tweet or Facebook tag them to the entire world. The best thing an aging musician (or any person for that matter) can do is smile. It is good to smile big and wide. Smile because you've lived this long, and loved this long, and hallelujah you're not the same for it. Smile because striving for the happiness of storybooks or American Idol, as well as finding all the elusive answers to the most un-ponderable things, has become less important than asking better questions. You smile because you believe in kindness but also in a little mischief. You smile because it will make others wonder how you do it. It is good to smile with a big, toothy, shit-eating grin and a swaggering neaner-neaner, because youth had its perks, better eyesight and higher breasts being just a couple, but age has come in on swan wings. It has glided in with fully stretched white feathers and finally come to rest on a clear silent pond. You smile because there are now more days than not that you don't feel the need to check your butt in the mirror before leaving the house, and it is nice. You smile for all that has vanished into the unreachable distance, and savor every sweet and salty lingering undertone.

Time is kinder to poets than to rockers, although it is true that the poet often goes unnoticed. Unnoticed because poetry rarely minces out on five-inch stilettos, or strides into the room all decked out in bravado and leather. The poet, if she is seen at all, will be watching a film of clouds pass over the moon; she may be weeping beside the three small stones unexpectedly found in an old cemetery at the edge of the woods. The poet is playing with a pun or is living more than a little mischief. She or he is dressed in corduroy, a warm jacket and muddy walking shoes. She may still wonder and ponder the strangeness of dimming vision, but she is cradling her hands and drinking from a fountain of newly-opened lilac blooms. She is smiling and weeping.

She is loving every little bit of it, every little bit – every single little bit of it.

Moments of Awe, Wonder & Holy Shit

October 2012

I read an article in *The New York Times* last week that reported on a scientific study created to prove that in moments of awe and wonder time appears to slow down. I must admit that I'm often amused by studies devised as a way to prove in a laboratory setting something most of us have known for a long time - intuitively and personally. I do acknowledge that sometimes these studies give us language and a way to talk about important issues or phenomena. I'm glad for this article and its affirmation of an intuitive and perhaps even mystical aspect of human experience. If asked, most people can tell you a story about such a moment. They can tell you how time slowed down, how the moment expanded in the way a deep breath expands our lungs. Most people can tell you of a leap of insight or a time when they felt a sense of peace, presence or connection. These experiences are not limited to the saints and poets, but something we all access, with practice and attention.

Our culture reasons that because we feel there is not enough time, we should increase our pace, multitask, and fit more into our already overbooked days. But even though it is counterintuitive to popular wisdom, perhaps the more effective response to the limits of time is to live more fully in the moment, to savor it and expand it. There is a sense of focus and clarity that happens when we do one thing well at a time. I'm as guilty as anyone in this modern age. I am often drawn into the headlong rush to work faster, instead of centering down and doing my best work. We are living at the crest of a wave of new technology that celebrates immediate connection, and yet we feel increasingly stressed out and alone. We cannot humanly get to the end of all our emails and so we walk around feeling pressed and vaguely worried. Most of us have lists of people who are "friends" on

Facebook or programmed into speed dial, but periodically I find myself asking, when was the last time I sat down with one of those speed dial folk for a real conversation over an unhurried meal? When was the last time I stopped, took a deep breath and really looked around? One of the perks of being a self-employed artist is that I can head into my office in the morning with a cup of coffee still in my pajamas. I can stop and look out the window, which in many ways is the first work of the poet. I can hang out all day with characters of my own imagining. I can stop and entertain a visiting muse when it sidles up to my writing desk. Side note: my muse never shows up looking like the fabled diaphanous muses of light and gossamer, but more often like a five year-old girl who dangles her feet and talks nonstop about this and that and that and this, and all the wonders of her day. Sometimes like a wise old swan that opens and flaps its white and grey wings, sending papers and feathers floating around the room. Occasionally, my muse shows up like the brief scent of lilacs or muddy ground. Sometimes it fills my office with the nostalgic smell of my mother's pot roast complete with greasy carrots and potatoes baked in a blue metal pan. And, on the most wondrous days, my muse shows up as an intense young poet who is so lost in thought, she doesn't even notice I'm there until I poke her in the ribs and she says, "Ah, yes, come with me, come further in, deeper, ever deeper, come, come and see." These are the good days, when I'm lost in making the ephemeral bit of language and moving air called song. I look out on the forest beyond my home as the sun is going down and I feel like I've been walking in a formed and unformed world of my own making. But on the dark days, I look out the window and the sun is hanging low and I'm still in my pajamas and I've never set foot in that wondrous world of making and muse. I've spent the whole today multitasking between Word documents and pdfs and email cues and mp3s and Facebook and Twitter and Tumblr and phone calls and a thousand websites. It is like there is a buzzing sound in my ears and head. I feel bad not just in my mind, but also in my whole body.

I know artistic obsession. It can be a beautiful focus that draws me out and into the work I love. But there is a dark side to obsession, and the pull of screens and endless communication has the dangerous feel of that dark side. So I've resolved to get away from my screens each day, put aside all the rings pings, blings and chimes of communication. Each day I'm building cairns. Cairns are collections of stones that people have traditionally left along road sides or paths to let the next traveler know that someone else has passed this way. They are an assurance that you are indeed still on the right trail, you are not lost, and that someone you do not know has wished you safe journey. They have a mysterious, almost magical feel to them. So lately I've been walking down to the pond and piling up a few stones by the water. I walk the wooded path behind my home and create little towers at this curve and then the next. I think what my heart is leaning into, the real purpose of creating these stacks of stones, is to remind me of my true journey, my real walk in this world, which has little to do with tangles of modern communication, wormholes of busy, and our culture's call to do more and more. Creating something of value and real depth requires me to dive deep, to get my fingers in the mud. When I do this, I might surface with shells, stones or bones. I may come back with a pearl or shining bit of agate. But it is impossible to do that kind of digging when I am only surfing on an ocean of disparate things. So each day I build another cairn to remind myself of a truer path, allowing my eyes to swing from side to side, looking for signs.

On Sunday evening I returned from a weeklong tour. As soon as I stepped into the house my husband, Robert, who struggles with his own type Triple A personality said, "Put down your bag! I love you, let's slow down and relax together, you know, like let's do a twenty-eight mile bike ride through the Morgan Monroe forest!" So we did, and peddling through the late autumn air we talked about gratitude, muses, and concerns about our old dog. We talked about Thanksgiving with his brother, and plans to see friends later in the week. In October, the Morgan Monroe Forest road is glorious. It is lined with bright yellow sassafras leaves, orange maples and locust, red oak and hickory. As you leave the park you get to cruise down a very long, steep hill. Robert, of course, lets gravity take him and he speeds down the hill with wide-open abandon. I tend to be cautious and ride my brakes a little on this particular hill. I like the momentum, but there is a blind curve at the bottom of the hill right before the park exit. But Robert grabs life with both hands, and I watched him zoom ahead. I knew he would be waiting for me to catch up at the next crossroad, sweaty and exhilarated. When I was nearly to the bottom of the hill I heard a sound. It was the rumble and deep hum of a very large motorcycle.

On a pretty autumn day, people will come from all over the state to cruise the beautiful back roads of Morgan, Monroe and Brown Counties. If you're so inclined you can bank awesome curves, slipping through the amber light, cruising atop a ton of finely tuned horsepower. When I came around the last blind curve there immediately in front of me was a procession of at least one hundred rumbling Harley Davidson motorcycles and riders, all out for a Sunday cruise as part of the Brown County Harley Davidson Jamboree. The Jamboree happens every fall. Thousands of Harley owners come from all over the region, converging on Brown County to ride their behemoth bikes, all covered with chrome and decked out with American flags. The riders have long grey ponytails and wear buckskin jackets with fringe, and there are lots of women over fifty sporting leather halter-tops. Right at the front of this ocean wave of revving engines, rounding the curve side by side, were two huge thundering motorcycles. They were occupying the entire road, one so far over into the left hand lane that I had to run my bike off the road and into the tall grass. Amazingly, I was able to quickly disengage my toe clips and did not dump my bike, but I had just barely escaped being directly hit by a motorcycle the size of a live rhinoceros.

Flashback – When Robert and I were traveling in India, we visited old Delhi, the most ancient section of Delhi. Old Delhi is a maze of narrow streets and shops that sell everything from fruit and spices to wedding dresses and brass statues, to stationary and bathroom fixtures. He'd told me a story about seeing a very elderly Sikh man make his way down one of the narrow roads. A young man on a motorcycle came careening around the corner and slammed on his brakes narrowly avoiding hitting this frail old man. Robert said what amazed him the most was not this narrowly averted accident, but rather to see the man's first reaction. The elderly man did not do the quick American response of a one finger salute, or shout, "You almost killed me, you fucking idiot!" The first response of this man was to press his hands together as if to pray and exclaim with sincerest gratitude, "God saved me." The first reaction of this man was not one of entitlement to safety or good fortune or even life. His first reaction was to be utterly grateful that even in a world of danger and sorrow, a world with no guarantees of good fortune or security, in that very moment he was safe and all right. That story has followed me through my days. It is a humbling and powerful image that has both inspired and haunted me. I've often wondered if I might ever reach such a place of enlightenment, where gratitude and love were always, no matter the circumstance, my first reaction.

Now we leave Old Delhi and come back to the back roads of southern Indiana, returning to a nearly flattened bicyclist and a road full of thundering motorcycles. I had just averted a terrible collision by running my bike off the road. I had bumped and slid to a stop shaking and my heart was racing. I had just avoided by mere inches being mowed down by a Harley Davidson the size of a black rhino. My first reaction, my very first reaction, was not to flip the rider off and shout, "You almost killed me, you fucking idiot!" But it still was not "God saved me." After years and years of reading Gandhi, and silent meditation, prayer beads and long walks. After studying Martin Luther

King, and reading and rereading Parker J. Palmer, Mary Oliver, Rilke and Merton, after a trip to India and a pilgrimage to Dharmsala, after all these years of thinking about and trying hard to practice love, compassion and nonviolence, my first knee jerk reaction was "Holy shit!!"

I realized immediately what I'd done, and I started laughing out loud. Ok, I've got some work to do and a ways to go, but "Holy shit" was not bad. I'm a musician who has toured for years with a bunch of guys in a minivan; I've bartended and worked in automobile factories; I'm the blue-collared daughter of Chicago South Side Italian immigrants. I was not raised in a monastery. No, it wasn't "God saved me," but maybe I might be inching up on an encouraging mile marker, a sign pointing the way, or at least a cairn-like indicator that I'm on the right road.

I grinned like a kid as the oblivious line of motorcycles rumbled by. The men in ponytails dipped their heads in greeting. The women riding behind them waved like prom queens in the autumn glow. They were blissfully unaware that the reason I was standing with my bike in the tall grass along the side of the road was not to marvel at the glory of sheer horsepower, but to calm my beating heart and shaky legs. So I waved back and grinned even wider, happy to be alive, grateful to be safe and maybe, just possibly, getting a little bit closer to the person I hope to be.

The Nature of Giving, Receiving & Lilac Bushes

I planted a lilac bush beside my home when I moved to this place four years ago. It is situated amidst an ever-expanding garden of perennials and what has become a bevy of bird feeders. I can see its glorious clusters of purple flowers through my bedroom window as I awaken, catching a hint of its unmistakable scent. Beyond the lilac bush, the deep green woods are filled with wildflowers bearing colorful local names like Trillium, Trout Lily, Jack-in-the-Pulpit, Solomon's Seal, and Jacob's Ladder. As you can tell, I have a great love for all things that flower and fly. But if I were asked to single out one bloom as my favorite, it would have to be the purple lilac. Many times I have buried my nose in clumps of them. I've lingered beside them on city streets, looking both ways before pinching a couple to take home or carry with me. I've tucked them behind an ear, in a shirt pocket or through a buttonhole. I have arranged them in vases or glasses of water, making humble living spaces smell extravagant.

With very few exceptions, I've planted lilacs in every place I've ever lived. I planted one next to the garage of the rented duplex where my daughter was born. I planted two in the front yard of the brick fixer-upper where my husband and I laid down the hardwood floors board-by-board. I planted one at a house by a lake and another next to a small apartment across from a park. I planted one beside a cracked sidewalk, another next to a vegetable garden, and one small twig of a thing alongside the water meter of an inexpensive walkup with linoleum floors and good light for painting. Because lilacs take several years to bloom, I have seen very few of those plants come to flower, even though I can imagine them all faithfully blooming each spring. I can envision a man slowing his pace as he catches the scent, or a woman greeted by their fragrance as she gets out of her car. I can see someone pause while washing dishes, a light breeze carrying that scent through an open kitchen window. I imagine an older woman cutting a few to bring inside just to brighten up the place, and a teenager looking both ways before pinching a few to take home or carry with him. I see them tucked behind ears, in shirt pockets or buttonholes, and arranged in vases and glasses of water. I can picture a person unconsciously perceiving the scent as it floats on the air, and when their heart feels lighter, they don't know why. I can even imagine someone giving the same blessing I've spoken myself when presented with blooms I did not plant: "Whoever you are, wherever you are, a blessing upon your head and heart."

Lilacs are old-fashioned flowers. They remind me of visiting my paternal grandparents, Calvin and Edna Newcomer. Grandpa was a twin, but his brother was born too small and did not live beyond a few days. He spoke to me only once of his brother, saying his tiny head could have fit in a teacup; his name was James. My grandfather did not go to school beyond the eighth grade, but he always had a stack of books from the library and his cherished *National Geographic* magazines beside his reading chair. He played the fiddle. He married my grandmother. He worked thirty years for the New York Central Railroad Line. Board-by-board he built their kitchen cabinets, and when he did not feel like listening, he turned off his hearing aid. He attended church every Sunday, went fishing religiously, and his backyard was filled with the fruit trees, gardens and lilacs he had planted. My grandmother's people were Indiana Amish folk by the name of Brenamen. She was raised by her older sisters after their mother was lost to the fever when Edna was only three years old. She named my father James Benjamin in remembrance of her father and Cal's brother. Her most prized possession was an image of a distelfink bird her mother had painted on a piece of good cloth. When times were tight, she worked as a cook for extra cash in the homes of the affluent. She canned tomatoes, corn relish, and bread and butter pickles, and put up pears and peaches in sweet, heavy syrup in blue mason jars. She embroidered elegant floral patterns in small, neat stitches on practical items such as dishtowels, tablecloths and handkerchiefs. She often smelled of rosewater, Lily-of-the-Valley, and lilacs, which she dabbed on her wrists from the five-and-dime perfume bottles she kept on her nightstand with her hand mirror, brush and comb.

My grandparents lived in a small city in a small house with a small yard, but together they created a Garden of Eden. I remember stepping outside; the whap of the screen door and the whitewashed wooden steps. In that moment, I was Dorothy Gale walking out the back door into the Technicolor Land of Oz. You see, my grandparents had planted every inch of their backyard with flowers, fruits and vegetables. There were corn, beans, strawberries, rhubarb and several types of fruit trees: apricot, plum and sour cherry. There was also a little pond where large, lazy goldfish swam and waited for the little bread balls we'd drop into the water for them to eat. Together my grandparents had created something glorious, useful and beautiful – all this and a lilac bush. And so it came to pass that New Eden was wrought by the hands of a railroad worker and a woman who cooked in other people's kitchens for extra money.

Calvin was first to pass beyond the veil of this world, and a few years later Edna followed him. I don't know if the next owners of that little house kept up the gardens. I figure, at least, the trees remain there, blossoming as reminders and giving the gifts of their best nature whether or not the fruit is put up in blue mason jars. I imagine there are still lilac bushes preserved like love letters written on good stationary with an old style fountain pen. In the course of our lives, we plant many things, assuming we will see the results of our work. We plant a row of tomatoes, expecting to eat them in mid-July. We put water on to boil, intending to drop in ripe corn immediately after it's been picked and shucked (which incidentally is the only sanctified way to eat Indiana sweet corn). Yarn that we bought in October is knitted into warm wool socks and then wrapped in Christmas paper. A baby conceived on New Year's Eve is born nine months after. The good chocolate we saved becomes a birthday cake. But despite the fact that we can and do see the literal fruits of our labor, so much of what we are and what we do moves out into the world like the scent of flowers on a warm spring day. We sing our songs, which are momentary and mostly made of air, light and our best intentions. We work for social, environmental and political change for the sake of our children's children. We are here and then we are gone. We bloom but for a season, leaving behind footprints and echoes, fruit trees and embroidered linens. We pass on a love for books and *National Geographic* magazine. We send out our songs like birds into the air and trust that these winged things will land safely enough. We give our children middle names that belonged to people we remember with great tenderness. We pass on the idea that it is honorable to give to an unknown recipient and that giving the best of ourselves was never designed to be a transaction with an equal balance sheet. We write love letters, we learn the names of wild flowers and birds, we build a life board-by-board, we plant lilac bushes and in moments of awareness and gratitude we raise our hands into the air and whisper, "Whoever you are, wherever you are, blessings upon your head and heart."

Love Notes and Yard Art

This is the short story that became the song "Forever Ray"

Janet Snopes stood up at the October meeting of the College View Neighborhood Association.

"It's an eyesore, it's tacky, and frankly it's just a little embarrassing, and I believe there may be a littering problem."

As usual, following any pronouncement by Janet, the room let out a collective sigh. The Snopes family had only recently moved to College View, but Janet was a woman of strong opinions concerning personal ownership and very quickly became one of the more vocal members of the group. College View Avenue was in an older section of town and within biking distance to Indiana University. The neighborhood had gone through many changes over the years, transforming from a vibrant neighborhood of young families, to a quiet street full of gradually aging owners to college student rental property. By the 1980's the area had fallen into sad disrepair with only small indicators of its former charm. Then in the financially optimistic days of the 1990's, a wave of style-conscious couples and families started buying up the shabby bungalows. They pulled up the shag carpet and refinished the oak floors. They stripped years of paint off the baseboards and moldings. They steamed away layers of wallpaper and fixed the leaky windows. They planted hydrangeas and hosta and spring daffodils to compliment the tall wide trees that graced the newly rebuilt sidewalks. After a semester of particularly noisy and party-prone students, a group of the homeowners formed the College View Neighborhood Association. They petitioned the city for stricter noise regulations and set up a neighborhood watch to discourage theft and vandalism. The cleaned up the alleys and pushed city government to begin recycling pick up. Eventually, most of the rentals returned to single-family ownership, and as the neighborhood became more quiet and safe, the College View Association had shifted its watchdog focus to other things. They focused on education, by bringing experts to speak at meetings on sustainability, weatherizing, environmentally friendly lawn care. They revived the annual summer block party, and many homes were now on the annual historic Bloomington and garden tours. But Janet Snopes was a woman who relished a good fight and had no trouble finding real or imagined wrongs to right. This month she had turned her gaze to Ella's front yard, just a bungalow and an alley away from her own. The meeting had gone late, and everyone knew that Janet could be a bit longwinded, so Sharon moved to adjourn and take up Janet's topic next month, and Ellen, the College View Association current President, quickly seconded the motion.

Ella's house was a green craftsman style bungalow situated at the corner lot of College View and University Street. It had a gracious and deep front porch. In the middle of a hard summer rain you could still sit out on the porch swing without getting wet. Ella was in her 90's and the only original owner still living in the neighborhood. Having passed through all the decline and revival, she was the neighborhood's most solid and eternally present soul. Ella and her husband Ray had built their house in 1947. They'd been married soon after Ray returned from military service. Ray had worked as an electrician at the Westinghouse plant from 1953 until he'd retired. Although they never had children of their own, all the original neighbors thought of them as family, kind of sideways relatives who lived just down the street. Ella was always good for a home baked cookie or on a hot summer day, a glass of red or green Kool-Aid tinkling with ice cubes pulled from her old metal ice cube tray. Ray was always on hand if a neighbor's circuit blew or to offer carburetor or electrical advice when groups of men still stood around cars with the hoods up and fixed them without the aid of computerized diagnostic tools. As they aged the neighborhood changed and there were not so many families, but they were still known, even by the renters, as the nice old people down the street. No one soaped their windows, slit their tires or turned over their garbage cans even when the neighborhood was at its rowdiest.

In 1985 Ray retired. He felt unfocused and a little at loose ends. He was restless in the way that only a man who has done physical work every day of his adult life can be. He puttered in his woodshop back in the garage. He read and reread his stack of *National Geographic* magazines. He tinkered around with the car and fixed the cord of an old toaster oven. One day he was hanging around the house, generally underfoot and driving Ella to distraction with endless household efficiency advice until she finally shooed him outside saying, "Ray, it's a lovely day, maybe there's some yard work you could do." Ray, a little put out and disgruntled, slumped out onto the porch. He surveyed the yard and garage and sidewalks. He had let the place go a little in the past few years. The old place could use a bit of sprucing up, and that was when he hatched his own home beautification plan. He put on his yard gloves and set to mowing the lawn. He then edged the grass at the sidewalk and stacked the fireplace wood more neatly next to the garage. At the end of the day he straightened his tired back and felt good about the visible difference he'd made in that one day. So in the coming weeks he pruned back the old lilac bush and mulched the flowerbeds. He thatched and reseeded the grass, fixed the gutter spouts and patched the cracks in the driveway. Finally after much determined beautification, Ray looked out at his tidy homestead and felt proud. Ray looked around at the declining neighborhood and thought to himself, "You know, what this neighborhood really needs is a little cheering up." So he went to a lawn ornament and garden shop out on the edge of town and returned with a larger than life cement rabbit. It was a dapper little statue sporting a waistcoat and britches, standing on its hind legs and offering a little waiter's tray with a flourish. He told Ella that he had picked out this rabbit because it reminded him of meeting her all those years ago, when she was a waitress at the Ladyman's Café downtown. He'd watched her pouring coffee and taking orders on a small waitress pad, with a stub of a pencil that she'd touch to her tongue before she began writing. She laughed easily, worked hard, and she had shoulder length wavy red hair, a regular hometown Rita Hayworth in a yellow waitress uniform. She had offered him a wide generous smile with her recitation of the lunch specials, and when she turned to place his order with the short order cook, he'd caught her scent of Shalimar perfume mixed with bacon and lemon meringue pie. He was smitten. After that, Ray spent way too much of his weekly pay on breakfasts and lunches he couldn't afford. He'd watch her carrying those plates of eggs, country ham and fried potatoes on a tray hitched up on her shoulder. When Ella heard the story and why he'd bought the little rabbit waiter lawn ornament, she smiled and hugged him long and hard around the neck. Ella loved the rabbit and every time she looked out the window she would remember how her own heart skipped a beat when she passed his table and how he'd wink at her when she was making coffee.

They started putting little things on the tray just for fun. They left peanuts still in the shell for the squirrels and birds, a cut flower from the garden. But soon, each morning, Roy began to leave Ella little notes on the tray. Ella would check in the late morning or early afternoon and find a bit of paper or 3x5 card weighted down by a small stone (so the note would not blow away). Ella loved returning from the grocery store or a meeting of her book club at the library, and finding there on the rabbit's tray a message just for her. The notes said things like; "Here's looking at you kid" and "To my honeybunch"; "Happy Birthday," "Happy Anniversary" and "Hot cha cha cha cha."
The notes were always signed with a smile, an L-shaped nose, three lines of hair standing straight up and two eyes, (one a dot, and the other a horizontal wink) and the signature "Forever Ray." After she read each note she would usually go find Ray and give him another hug around the neck.

This was how Ella and Ray began collecting yard art. Regularly they would visit the statuary store out on the bypass. They brought home a momma duck and five small ducklings because it reminded them of the pond at Ray's parents' old farm. They bought two kissing Dutch children in honor of Ella's maternal grandmother and grandfather who had come over from Holland with nothing but a suitcase and a sewing machine. They put out a cement collie dog that stood at faithful attention to honor Blondie who brought in their paper and slept at the foot of the bed for 15 years. They bought a gnome with a staff, an impressive Big Foot and sheriff Andy Griffith to protect the house when the neighborhood was in its roughest phase. Their purchases began to get bigger and eventually Ray borrowed a flat bed truck and brought home a life-sized angel with open hands and bare feet. Once after Easter Sunday service together they picked out and brought home a sweet-faced Madonna. Ella said she like the lady, because if she were to be completely honest, God had always seemed so big and bossy, and Jesus was just too perfect and every hair in place. But she'd always thought that Mary, with her passel of kids, laundry to hang and dinners to cook, was someone a person could actually sit down with for that occasional important heart to heart. One Memorial Day they brought home the poured concrete shoes of a solider, which they placed near the orange Tiger Lilies. Ray recited the names of some his friends who had not made it home from the war all those many years ago: Jim Berman, Carl Hanover, Lee Richey and Thomas Kelly. He pulled out his pocket-handkerchief, wiped his eyes and blew his nose. He and Ella stood there quietly, hand in hand, while the evening gathered. They continued collecting yard statuary. Each piece was a remembrance, an image that delighted or comforted. They were sentinels and protectors, wry winks and nods to one memory or another. And, every morning, rain or shine, Ray faithfully left a small note on the tray of the rabbit waiter, which stood in the place of honor at the center of the yard.

Today Ella is looking out the window at the wide winged angel, and at her always affable Madonna. She likes to sit here in the sunlight with her morning tea and enjoys watching how the morning light rests so gently on all those familiar images. Ray passed last year. He slipped away quietly after a bout of pneumonia. He had gotten over the illness, but it had taken too much out of him. Ella remembered how folks used to call pneumonia "the old people's friend." Ray had been basically good humored and blessedly healthy, but his body had become like a pocket watch that had been wound so often and for so long that the springs and small gears just couldn't hold onto the true time anymore. No shock or momentary panic of heart attack or long drawn-out cancer, just a finally letting go, a gradual quieting of the breath. She remembers how after the memorial service she'd gotten down a number of shoeboxes secured with a bit of string from the hall closet. She had tenderly cut the string with her little sewing scissors, and inside were hundreds of little notes, 3x5 cards and love letters – each and every one signed with a grin and a wink and "Forever Ray."

She had read them all.

She reread them again.

Then she had kissed each one, and put it back in a shoebox.

Now every morning she goes out to the rabbit, and places her own note on the tray. But unlike Ray she places no stone to hold it there.

She just lets the wind carry them, sending them lifting down the street, and out into the world.

Wednesday, on her way to the doctor, Janet found a piece of paper in the holly bush next to her front door. She picked it out of the sticky leaves and read, "Don't be afraid." On Thursday, while walking her dog, she caught a note that was tripping down the down the street. It said, "You're right where you need to be." Gavin the UPS driver stepped out of the truck in front of Janet's house. He picked up a small card lying on the sidewalk. He read, "There is still wonder in the world." It's been propped up on his dashboard ever since. On Friday, Janet pulled into her driveway and found a wet 3x5 card sticking to the front porch steps. All it said was, "It will be alright. It just takes time." She looked down the street, the late autumn wind whipping down from the corner of College View and University Avenues.

At the November Campus View Neighborhood Association Meeting, Janet Snopes made no motion or disparaging comments about Ella's front yard – or ever again for that matter. And since then, each week, she brings Ella a pie or casserole. Ella always pours them a little tea and they talk about the notes and what they mean. Janet sends her teenage son to shovel the walks when it snows, and once in a while she places her own note on the tray. But what she writes upon those bits of paper is a story for another day.

The Caterpillar and Moth

or the more you know…the more you don't know

I was listening to a radio program the other day that described the life of a caterpillar and its transformation into a butterfly or moth. Essentially, the caterpillar snuffles along its lumpy way eating its fill, extending itself little by little bit. Because, well, because it is a caterpillar's nature to rumple the world and to be rumpled by it. But eventually, the caterpillar has snuffled and eaten enough for one caterpillar life, and so it wraps itself into a solitary womb called the cocoon or chrysalis. As soon as it is settled into this secret place, it immediately breaks down into its gooey elements. Really. I'm not kidding. I always thought the caterpillar must go through a process similar to the B-movie version of human to werewolf, with the parts of the moth erupting and elongating from the body. But the truth is even stranger than B-movie fiction. Between the life of the bumbly caterpillar and the elegant butterfly or moth there is a middle time when the caterpillar becomes a middle thing that is unrecognizable as critter or even critterish. In that middle time, the caterpillar goes back into all the elements from which it came. It breaks down to a cellular, atomic level. From dust it came and to dust it returns. Then, and only then, when it has let go of everything wonderful and fine and hard and toilsome about its rumpled caterpillar days, it grows into its new self, rearranging all those liquid elements into the paper thin wings, delicate antennae, and graceful long legs of its moth or butterfly form.

But wait, there's more miracles and magic. Scientists have determined that the moth or butterfly, that entirely new creation, remembers what it was before its transformation. A moth or butterfly will react to significant experiences remembered from its earthbound former life. The scientists described exposing a caterpillar to an unpleasant smell, which they linked to an unpleasant feeling. Eventually the caterpillar would react adversely when it encountered the smell again. When the newly transformed moth was reintroduced to the same unpleasant smell, the moth reacted. Yes, the memories, events, and experiences of that caterpillar's days carried forward. Something of the caterpillar's first self survived through the middle unformed, elemental, unrecognizable-as-a-critter phase. But wait, there's still more. Science folk have also found that if you look carefully through a microscope into the body of a caterpillar, there are teeny tiny elemental bits of the foreshadowed wings and butterfly body parts. Somehow, when the caterpillar becomes goo, those precious bits are safely tucked aside through all the melting and breaking down, and brought into the process when reassembling and reforming.

So here's the thing that has been following me since hearing that podcast – there is something of the future butterfly or moth patiently waiting in the caterpillar's deepest secret places. It is carried like a promise, like a question, ok...like a soul. And there is also something of the caterpillar's knowledge, wisdom, and rumpled caterpillar life that is carried forward into its new and transformed moth or butterfly self.

The persistence of the caterpillar's memory after its breakdown and reforming, and the small secret presence of the moth or butterfly foreshadowed wings within the body of the caterpillar, leads me to ponder. What wisdom or image of my future self do I carry now within my secret heart? What promise or question or spirit within me is waiting for the right moment to fly? When I transform, and I will transform throughout my life (and perhaps even after this life), what of my former self will carry through? Perhaps those experiences that have broken me down to my barest self are not ends but means to a new becoming. Perhaps the caterpillar and the moth are not either/or propositions, and in turn, perhaps I am not....nor are we.

In the Sitka Pines

Alaska, 2012

On Saturday, March 19th I had the opportunity to take a walk through an old growth Sitka Pine Forest. The trees were very tall and quiet, and the wide trail was lined with ancient totems made by the Tlingit peoples of southeastern Alaska. Cindy, a tall windswept woman who was my guide on this hike, showed me a stream that wound inland from the seawater of the Sitka Sound to mix with the fresh water of the island. She told me that soon this stream would be filled with spawning salmon, so full that bank to bank would be a solid blanket of fish. She went on to tell me that these salmon had all been born in that stream. They had grown to viable size and then swam out into the ocean. The Sitka salmon travel great distances, some as far as the coast of Japan. But eventually, when the time is right, something mysterious begins to call them home, and they all return to the very stream where they were born (all but 1%, which is the correct amount to keep the gene pool strong). They spawn in the place they were born and then they die. I commented to my guide, "How sad that these fish should travel so wide, know so many miles of ocean, come so far only to return and die." She smiled at me and looked back down into the streambed and said, "Ah, but you don't understand. When this generation of salmon die they put into the streambed exactly the right nutrients, in exactly the right proportions to help the new salmon hatch and grow to ocean-sized viability." She went on to tell me that the minerals and elements of all the oceans these salmon have traveled is taken into their bodies and when they die those important elements are brought home and given to the next generation, and to the land, the trees and other living things of the island. Something lives and something dies, the salmon transform and their lives continue – just in a new form.

This is a powerfully important story. We live and lose and live again.

Those we love and have passed from mystery into mystery are not gone, but they are transformed. They are in everything and all around us. They live in the ocean and in the dappled woods, they live in the sunlight and moonlight, they live in our hearts and memory. They live in our very bones.

In a moment all is transformed. Nothing is ever truly lost.

Yes

March 1993

I am sure it left through her fingertips. She'd been sleeping in the deep Barcalounger while I held one hand and my father held the other. Her nails were blue by then, and the sky had changed from black to grey, from grey to rose color. I thought to myself, "Now." I knew how terribly afraid she'd been to die in the dark. I didn't understand this fear; I'd always felt the night had mysteriously open arms, but my mother was an extremely private woman, and there was much about her I'd never know or understand. She breathed out a long, punctuated sigh, like ellipses at the end of a sentence.

She was, and then she wasn't.

It was like Time stood quietly aside, not wanting to disturb us, allowing the seconds to slow and then stop, out of respect for our bewilderment. No one in the awakening town would notice that the world was forever changed, or that the succession of moments had stopped in one small living room with a long eastern view. My father looked up at the ceiling and said, "I suppose she's up there listening." It did seem to me she'd stopped and waited midair as the veil between the worlds drew aside, hovering just a little longer until she left us with the sound of "Yes."

November 1982

Nine months and two weeks had passed; all the while, she had rested in the deep Barcalounger chair of my body, humming contentedly, hearing every song I knew, connected to me by every heartbeat and breath. And yet, in her round, astonished eyes, I saw a new person saying, "Now that was something." She had become a manifested soul who would walk, and then inevitably walk away.

The umbilical cord was, and then it wasn't.

Her little hand curled around my finger. The midwives cooed, and when she cried, I swear to God it sounded like the bleating of a lamb in the field. The awakening town would not notice that time had slowed and then come to a satisfied, shimmering stop in one small living room with long southern windows, or that I had labored through the night until the sky had turned from black to grey, from grey to rose color, until there could be no more waiting, until there was nothing but the sound of "Now," and then "Yes."

Christmas 1965

Amid much whispering and shushing, my excitable little sister, and saint-in-training older sister, pushed me into my parents' bedroom. I tapped on my mother's shoulder, smiling my best and most sincere smile. "Honey, are you up already? Are the others awake too?" I nodded my best and most sincere nod. My father began to stir, and my mother said, "Christmas starts at the crack of dawn this year, Jim." My father opened one eye, took in my most sincere smiling and nodding self, rumbled a moan and rolled over. My mother leaned over and brushed the hair out of my eyes with the tips of her fingers, "Go wait at the top of the stairs, dear." Soon my plaid-flannel father and my rose-patterned mother emerged from the bedroom. Raising his hand in parental blessing, we ran down the stairs like rain sliding down the roof and over the awning. No one in our awakening town would know that in one small living room, in the glow of bubble lights reflecting in clumps of tinsel scatted on the lower half of a pine tree, time skipped a beat. My sisters began shaking packages, but I stood at the entrance to the room hovering a little midair. At only six going on six and a half, I sensed, but could not know, that time stops rarely in one's life.

Some things are, and then they aren't.

My little sister breathlessly said, "Now?"

My mother looked out the eastern window at the sky that had gone from black to grey, from grey to rose and said, "Yes."

Heart and Bones

I discovered recently that throughout our lives our bones and teeth become reservoirs for the chemical elements to which we are exposed. Our bodies use the local water we drink to form the proteins and elements present in our hair, fingernails, muscles and other body tissues. I have always believed that we spiritually and emotionally carry our landscapes with us; in fact, when I cross the Monroe County line something in my spirit sighs, "yes," and "home." But I have been taken with the idea that the land and water of our homes quite literally become a part of us physically. The spirit of a place gets into our hearts and souls, and the basic elements of a place essentially are joined to our very bodies and bones. I live in a place the land maps call by many names: North America, the Midwest, the state of Indiana, the Ohio River Valley, Monroe County, Bloomington, New Unionville and Penitentiary Hollow. I have called this place I live by all of these names including descriptions like: "down the road from Mary's mule pastures," "around the bend from Allen's gardens" and "across from Bill and Sue's place." But the name I most often use is "home."

Being a musician and songwriter, I travel a great deal, so I've come to deeply appreciate my moments resting in the arms of place that I've now learned has been physically incorporated into my body and bones. I remember a long tour that happened to follow the movement of springtime from south to north. I started in Corpus Christi, Texas driving through fields of bluebonnets on the way to Austin. I traveled up through the blooming vines of Carolina wisteria and the white dogwoods of the Shenandoah Valley. I ended up breathing in the yellow forsythia and new violets of New England and upstate New York. About halfway through this tour, I began to feel lonesome and hungry. Although each area was beautiful and wondrous in its opening into a new growing season, all I wanted was the familiar sights and scents of southern Indiana in the springtime. I began to dream about the wooded path behind my home. I dreamt of purple redbuds and white dogwoods so soft and vibrant against a veil of tiny light spring green leaves. I kept looking for the familiar wildflowers we call by local names; May Apples, Trillium, Trout Lilies, Wild Phlox, Jack-in-the-Pulpits and Dutchman's Britches. I longed for the sight of new growth in the muddy Indiana clay. I kept waiting for the damp smell of local leaves (poplar, maple, beech, oak and ash) that fall here in the autumn, returning to the ground in just the right proportion to foster the new seedlings. The very elements of the land and water I know so intimately as home were calling me back. I remember returning to Indiana after that long springtime tour. I remember putting down my guitars in the middle of the driveway, walking back into the woods behind my house getting down on my hands and knees and pressing my nose deep into the leaves and moss. In that ancient posture of prayer and gratitude I breathed in the rich scent of growing things. Rumi said it, "There are a thousand ways to kneel and kiss the ground." But that day, there could be no metaphor, only real mud on the knees of my jeans. I took a little bit of moss and leaves, a wild violet and a snail shell into the house. I carried them around with me for most of that day, and every so often breathed in a little bit of that rich Indiana dirt. With every deep breath my heart said, "Home" and my bones said, "Yes."

Arthur B and Bob

From the Betty's Diner Collection - inspiration for the song "Arthur B and Bob"

Arthur B and me are very good friends. I love Arthur B and Arthur B really really loves me. Arthur B and Libby-dearest picked me out of a hard-worried cage. Libby-dearest smiled and said I was a fine retriever-hound-cocker-spaniel-brown dog and this made me very proud. They took me home and away from the hard-worried cage and now my name is Bob, which is a fine name, and I am a good and grateful dog.

Libby-dearest gave me biscuits and let me jump up in the big bed and called me Slobber-Bobber and she smelled so so so good. She laughed a lot and danced in the living room with the shiny bell on her fingers. Libby-dearest's shiny bell dancing made Arthur B a little nervous, but I could tell it made Arthur B a little proud. Before Libby-dearest went away she stopped shiny bell dancing and slept and slept and dreamed and dreamed and smelled like something worried. Arthur B sat next to her and I sat next to Arthur B while she dreamed and dreamed. Now I take care of Arthur B so he is not alone in the big wide worried world with dogs and cars and buildings and no shiny bell dancing Libby-dearest smell. When Arthur B is sad we are sad together. One night I howled for sad and Arthur B howled for sad, and we howled for sad together in the dark worried night. Arthur B is thin and he forgets to eat and once he forgot to put food in my good-dog bowl and he felt very very sorry and he cried no Libby-dearest no shiny bell dancing tears. I didn't mind even though an empty good-dog bowl is a sad thing. I love love love to go for a walk with Arthur B and sometimes we go to the nice lady cold hamburger place where he ties me up outside and tells me to guard the parking meter, which is a very important job and I am a good and grateful dog. I can see Arthur B through the window and the nice lady brings him things to eat and sometimes she brings me cold hamburger pieces. Cold hamburger pieces are the best best best food in all all all the world. One night when Arthur B was sad the nice lady brought me inside and I put my head on his knee under the table so he would know that he was not alone in the big worried world. I love Arthur B and Arthur B loves me and I am a good and grateful dog.

Fishing with Ron and Ed

Bits of this story appear in the song "I Do Not Know Its Name" and "Shine"

In August I facilitated a writing workshop at a retreat center that could best be described as a "progressive theological dude ranch." Yes, proving you can't make up things like real life – imagine, twenty-five Unitarians on horseback. It was marvelous. This retreat center is called Ring Lake Ranch and it is situated in the Wind River region of the Grand Teton Mountains, which is an area that the native peoples have called sacred for literally thousands of years. The rocks are covered with winged petroglyphs, some believed to be at least 4,000 years old. There is something that happens to a person upon entering a landscape of such scale. In southern Indiana we measure change in days or seasons. We mark the time by the first appearance of ripe corn at the farmer's market or when the tulip poplars' leaves turn from green to yellow. But in the Wind River region time is measured by the effect of wind and water upon stone over the course of centuries. Standing in a landscape of that scale we can sense that the days of our lives are but moments of light on the surface of a lake. All is immediate, and all is transient. It was at Ring Lake Ranch that I met Ed and Ron, two Methodist pastors from Rhode Island and California, both avid catch-and-release fly fishermen. There are people who fish and then there are fly fishermen. Ed can tell you minute details about water currents, the effects of weather on mayfly hatch, and the mysterious ways of the lake trout. Ron is a quiet man and also deeply knowledgeable of the natural world. One evening at dinner, Ed and Ron offered to teach me how to throw a fly line. So the next morning I borrowed waders from my friend Cindy and soon found myself standing with these two men, hip-deep in glacial lake water, learning the nuances of fly casting. If you have not seen an experienced fly fisherman in action it's really pretty amazing. They use a light rod and a weighted line. Attached to the end of the line is a marvelously hand-tied fly, meticulously made to simulate mayflies or other insects that trout find most tasty. An experienced fly fisherman will cast out his line in slow, graceful whipping motions, which allows an increasing length of line to be fed into the air. The line slowly and gracefully lengthens, creating a lazy looping pattern that looks like a moving infinity symbol. This line catches the sunlight, flashing all around the fisherman, a miracle of motion and light and 10 lb. trout line.

As we stood in that cold clean lake, Ron told me that he thought fly fishing was a wonderful metaphor for the spirit of God moving in his life. He knew in his heart that something quiet and beautiful was always moving just below the surface. He told me that the spirit of God was like the big fish you longed to see so much that you'd stand waiting for hours, tossing out your line again and again, often in all the wrong or foolish places. But occasionally, once in a lovely while, you would catch a glimpse of that spirit. You might even get to hold it in your hands for just a moment. But, because the spirit of God is a wild and mysterious thing, you had to let it go. Experiencing the living spirit was not always predictable, but it was always wondrous and worth the wait. Right after Ron told me this lovely metaphor, the end of his fishing rod bent completely down. Something huge had hit. His eyes brightened and he began the slow process of letting out the line and reeling it in. You do this because if you try to reel a large fish (and this had to be a very large one) too quickly the thin line would break. Ron stayed with the fish, allowing it to run and coaxing it back in, and after about 20 minutes of give and take, release and pull, he saw it. His eyes grew wide, "Holy Jesus on a soda cracker!" (which is the raciest expletive a pastor can utter in mixed company). It was the largest lake trout he'd ever seen. It was enormous and shining. Its sides flashed silver and it was very strong. Eventually, with Ed's help, they slowly reeled the big fish into the shallows. Ron and Ed held it there in the water, running their hands over its sides so tenderly and respectfully. They held it just so because it was too big for even their largest net. They called it by lovely names like "Good Friend," and "Beautiful Fish," and "Old Man." And finally, when they were sure that wonderful creature was not too tired, and after they were sure its strong gills were working properly, they let it go. They let it go.

But this is what happened. And this, my friend, is true. When that beautiful fish made its way out into the deep water, before it dove down into the unknowable depths, its tail and long body were making and unmaking the shape of a question mark.

County Fairs and Chicken Ears

The song "I Wish I May, I Wish I Might" grew out of this essay

I went to the Monroe County Fair with my friend Faith last week. Faith is a New Testament theologian who grew up in New York. She has a wickedly brilliant sense of humor and extensive collection of tacky Jesus paraphernalia. My personal favorite of her collection is a hard-won church basement bingo game treasure, a wall clock with a scene of The Last Supper on its face that heralds each hour with a message from one of the twelve apostles saying things like, "Hi, I'm Peter. Jesus called me while I was fishing with my brothers Andrew and James. It is now one o'clock." There will be more about the importance of Faith's expertise as a biblical scholar and her affinity for Jesus collectibles later in this story. We had decided to go to the fair because a mutual friend's daughter had just won several 4-H prize ribbons for her heirloom breed chickens. Melissa's daughter is a quiet young woman who loves and cares for her chickens with incredible devotion, and with great knowledge and appreciation of the fine nuances of chicken inner workings. So, for love and poultry, we ventured into the belly of the Monroe County Fair beast, where we checked out the goat barn, marveled at the actual size of pig butts and watched hopeful farm kids proudly lead their washed and combed sheep into the judging ring.

Eventually we made our way to the poultry tent to make oohing and ahhing sounds over Alison's chickens, which had many colorful ribbons pinned to the outside of their cages. I was thrilled and amazed to find out from our proud and knowledgeable poultry guide that chickens have two stomachs. I also learned that you could actually tell what color egg a chicken will lay by the color of its ears: red ears indicate brown eggs and green ears indicate white eggs. I was taken in by the poetry of this fact. Melissa said it would be best to double-check this information on the Internet. Faith, being a professionally trained theologian, would not blindly take chicken revelation for gospel until showed and convinced that chickens actually do have ears.

After we'd enjoyed all things chickens for a good long while, Faith and I decided to take a stroll up the dusty fair midway. We grabbed something to drink at the lemon shake-up booth, but passed on purchasing one of the eight hundred versions of fried dough available. Indiana fairs, like many state and county fairs, unveil a glorious new fried food each year. Past delicacies included fried Moon Pie, fried Snickers and Twinkies, fried Pepsi Cola (I swear I am not making this up) and fried butter (which is wrong on too many levels to count). While we meandered the midway we noticed a long line of people waiting to enter the main event pole barn. The line stretched out and reached all the way past the Scrambler and almost to the Tilt-A-Whirl, and consisted of adults bouncing babies on their hips or pushing them in strollers. We finally asked one young mother why everyone was waiting in line. The incredulous response was, "You don't know?" And then with an air of prideful assurance, "Well, tonight is the night of the Monroe County Most Beautiful Baby Contest." Yes, Beloved, each and every single parent and grandparent waiting in that enormous line was sure without a shadow of a doubt that they were holding in their arms the most beautiful child ever born. These are humble Midwestern folk, and many of these parents would never imagine entering any other kind of contest. The woman in the flowered sundress might make a mean coconut cream pie, but would not venture to enter it in the pie and cake gala, or the tall fellow with the Dekalb Corn baseball cap might tool wonderful wooden toys but would never consider submitting them in the arts and crafts competition. The young mother in the "I'm in the Swine Club" T-shirt was in all likelihood a woman who, when complimented on a job well done, would brush aside the compliment and say, "I had a lot of help." The parents were tall, short, round, thin, white, Latino, African

American, fashion dos and fashion dont's, waiting in line in the waning heat of that summer evening. They carried baby girls in bonnets and lace, little boys in OshKosh B'gosh overalls and checkered shirts, they jiggled pacifiers and kept the sun off the ones sleeping in push chairs. They cradled them in proud, sunburned arms, or hitched them up on swaying hips. It was a wonder of love and confidence. And as Faith and I proceeded down the midway, I held the firm conviction that yes, there is only one most beautiful child ever born, and it belongs to each and every mother and father.

After marveling at Monroe County's extraordinary abundance of beautiful babies, Faith and I were joined by Melissa and another friend, Michelle. Together we wandered over to the commercial display building, which was full of booths set up by local businesses and organizations, like the Monroe County Public Library, Bloomington Animal Shelter, La Leche League, various Democratic and Republican candidates, hot tub installers and animal feed dealers. Sprinkled among these organizations and businesses were booths run by local churches. The church booths were mostly attended by sincere pastors, ladies of the church, and bored, young people roped into the job by their enthusiastic youth group leaders. One particular church announced its modern appeal with a fancy touch screen machine that bore a sign reading "Bible Quiz and Contest." I had to wonder how many youth group car washes and Silver Saints knitting and bake sales it took to purchase an item of such worth and evangelizing potential. I looked at my friends and said, "Heck, between the four of us, we have a New Testament biblical scholar (and former Jeopardy contestant), a teacher raised on Southern Baptist Bible drills, a former good Catholic girl, and a Quaker folksinger (who was excellent at quietly being supportive). We could easily clean up on this game and win the free Bible tract or maybe even the grand prize, Jesus-walks-on-the-water snow globe. So we decided to take a whirl at the Bible quiz and proceeded to have entirely too much fun arguing about the finer points of Bible knowledge. An elderly and very sincere pastor watched as we decided whether Noah's ark was made of Cyprus or gopher wood, high-fiving one another when it was the women, not the boys, to whom Jesus first appeared in the garden. The preacher was rather impressed at our consistently high scores as we approached the final lightning round of the hardest questions. The pastor confided that we were scoring better than a local minister who had just come by with his wife. The wife had boldly stated that her husband would surely get a 100% score because the Holy Spirit teaches him everything he needs to know about scripture without ever actually reading the Bible. It was reported that the local minister with the confident wife finished with a 32% score and had to slink away without even a free Bible tract. Holy Spiritual guidance aside, we were on a winning roll with the coveted snow globe in sight. So we pressed on and finished the lightning round with an 80% correct score. A little crowd had gathered around the touch screen machine. Something exciting was happening at the Baptist booth. The bored youth group kids had stopped texting their friends, and some of the women were smiling appreciatively and nodding. Our very sincere pastor asked if we all had "church homes," but took a little step back when I explained Faith was a Princeton-trained New Testament Theologian but not so much into substitutionary atonement theology, Michelle was a Catholic-turned-Methodist but regularly consulted a numerologist, Melissa was raised Southern Baptist in Texas (he breathed a little sigh) but now taught Unitarian Sunday School (he took the breath back in). And I was a silent Quaker. I told him that Quakers may have read the Bible, but we were just very quiet about it. He did not laugh.

I am sorry to say we did not win the Bible quiz contest. The last question did not have a single multiple-choice option that satisfied us all, so we left it blank and left without Bible tract or snow globe. But I did hear from one of the disappointed youth that we should come back next year, because they were planning on upping the grand prize to a whole collector's edition of "Scenes of The Exodus Snow Globe Series," a marvelous set incorporating teeny tiny locusts, frogs, flies, and hail instead of snow. The four of us know that this may just be an exciting rumor, but we're brushing up on our plague knowledge, just in case.

I am miles away and many years from the county fairs where my sister and I held hands as we rounded the apex of the Ferris wheel, and waved to my mother from the center of a spinning teacup. I can close my eyes and still taste how delicious it was to be thirteen years-old driving a brightly painted bumper car, chased by the boy who made my heart beat like thunder. But this year's fair held its own charm, like a lemon shake-up cup overflowing with beautiful babies, extraordinary chickens, local country bands, funnel cakes and elephant ears. My friends and I went to the fair for love and poultry and left amid a crowd of teenagers in tank tops and cut off shorts, carrying pink, purple and green stuffed animals won by tossing beanbags into a box. As we walked slowly toward the fallow soybean field being used for fairground parking, we smiled at the farm kids bedding down their goats, ponies and lambs. And in the red glow of a wide Indiana sunset, we nodded to tired parents, each carrying the most beautiful child ever born, fast asleep with its tender head resting lightly upon their proud shoulders.

Kappy's Cow

My friend Kappy has a cow named Vista. She loves this cow with great tenderness and the knowing amusement of an inside joke. Each rose-tinged morning and indigo evening Kappy coaxes creamy milk from Vista's plentiful udder. Kappy draws long open-handed strokes down Vista's broad bovine side. She mixes this companionable affection with Vista's alfalfa, oats and feed corn. In return, Vista bestows upon this woman a steady brown gaze, the smell of dusty hay, and stainless steel buckets of body-warmed gratitude. Both woman and cow consider this to be an affable arrangement, a contract based in contentment. I followed Kappy into the barn wearing her teenage son's oversized chore boots. The October air was crisp and clean and a silent horned owl flew across the Wisconsin moon on its mortally quiet wings. There are no mice near this barn, filled with working barn cats who take their commission to guardianship quite seriously. When the milking is done, Kappy fills and sets out two saucers. The calicos, greys, and long-tailed tigers gather around. They are purring loudly and full of themselves. They are regal and fierce, so protective of the oats that Vista ruminants into milk somewhere in the secret compartments of her four stomachs. Kappy washes the emptied udder while Vista finishes her grain, and just for a moment she leans her head down, pressing her forehead into the comfort of a contented cow. "It was a long summer," she says, "hot and dry and forever with the letting go of it." I nod and look out the barn door, at the full moon, at the stand of trees, at the sheep and dogs that look up and sniff the wind for any hints of change.

I know that tomorrow Kappy will pasteurize Vista's milk in a clean container next to her kitchen sink. She will distribute chilled glass gallon jars to her neighbors. Sometimes she trades the milk for handmade soaps or chicken feed, but mostly she gives it away without fanfare or flourish. She is happy just knowing her neighbor children's bones are growing stronger. Vista is good at being a cow, and she also does this without extra credit.

Kappy is good at loving her cow. In that hay-scented barn, in the chill of October, I still can believe that the extraordinary motions of love are the most ordinary and predictable of occurrences. The night hunters hunt, and the cats puff themselves up, but the ruminations of love and generosity persevere. As long as the moon shines full in a Midwestern sky, as long as a kind woman can still love a good cow, there is infinite reason to believe.

Credits & Appreciation

Thank you to Robert for understanding the difference between what is real and what is true, and for saying, "Why not?" and "Leap in," and always being a safe place to land.

To the wild women (Faith, Michelle, Melissa and Krista) in my ongoing prose/poetry writing group. Thank you for believing in my words and hearing me in to speech. Thank you to Parker and Sharon. Our deep and honest conversations were at the heart of many of these poems and essays. Much appreciation to Amelia, who ponders the nuances of living with me, and gets my sideways sense of humor. To Ben, who always gives me something new to ponder. To Jill, for inspiration and floating in the pond imagining a better world.

Thank you to Gary and Jim, and everyone who has sojourned this wide world with me. Many of these songs and poems grew out of experiences on the road and conversations in rental cars, at airports, and backstage before shows.

My great appreciation to friends and family, good people and kind folks I meet and work with everywhere I go.

And of course to Ericka and Tim and Mike and Lorel and Kappy and Hugh and Cate, and all the folks who help me organize my permeable poet's life.